DATE DUE

❧ **Gift** ❧
Young Adult/Children's Books
Examination Center
of
Missouri State Library
Jefferson City, MO

CMSU 181-84

C0-ARK-069

CHILDREN'S AND YOUNG ADULTS
BOOK EXAMINATION CENTER
MISSOURI STATE LIBRARY

520795

The Little Witch's Carnival Book

by Linda Glovach

Prentice-Hall, Inc., Englewood Cliffs, N.J.

MISSOURI
THE UNIVERSITY
Warrensburg,
Missouri

WITHDRAWN BY
JAMES C. KIRKPATRICK LIBRARY
TECHNICAL SERVICES

For Spotty, Nicky, Spencer,
Morgan, and Mom . . .

Copyright © 1982 by Linda Glovach
All rights reserved. No part of this book may be
reproduced in any form, or by any means, except for
the inclusion of brief quotations in a review,
without permission in writing from the publisher.
Printed in the United States of America   • J
Prentice-Hall International, Inc., London
Prentice-Hall of Australia, Pty. Ltd., North Sydney
Prentice-Hall of Canada, Ltd., Toronto
Prentice-Hall of India Private Ltd., New Delhi
Prentice-Hall of Japan, Inc., Tokyo
Prentice-Hall of Southeast Asia Pte. Ltd., Singapore
Whitehall Books Limited, Wellington, New Zealand

10 9 8 7 6 5 4 3 2 1

Library of Congress Cataloging in Publication Data
Glovach, Linda. The little witch's carnival book.
    SUMMARY: Simple instructions for putting on a
carnival in the back yard or inside the house, with
costumes, hats, food, games of chance, and sideshow.
    1.   Children's parties—Juvenile literature.
2.   Amusements—Juvenile literature.   3.   Creative
activities and seat work—Juvenile literature.
[1.   Parties]   I.   Title.
GV1205.G57   793.2'1   81-19260
ISBN 0-13-538074-X   AACR2

JE
793.21
G5184 LW

Contents

520795

Introduction

Welcome to the carnival! Since it is a special Little Witch carnival, it's not exactly like other carnivals; however, there are lots of games that tell your future and your fortune, there are prizes, and lots to eat. If you don't like witch burgers, there are spooky pops and crunchy popcorn.

There are tickle sticks to make for the guests and tall top hats for the booth workers. And there are money boxes to keep your profits in.

Later on, if you like, there are a sideshow and a raffle. You can see it all through colored carnival glasses!

Little Witch's Carnival Code

Look at this list whenever you need to be reminded of the general carnival rules.

1. Make a list of all the material and food ingredients you will need. Purchase them in advance and have things made and ready the day of the carnival. Food and beverages can be made the night before or the morning of the carnival.

2. Make sure your invitations and billboards are sent out and evenly scattered about. Be sure to set a rain date for the near future on your signs.

3. It is a good idea to pick your performers for the sideshow and start rehearsing a few days before the carnival.

4. Make enough of everything—and even extras—so you don't run out.

5. Have an adult nearby to help if anything gets difficult. The manager's job is to check around to make sure everything is running smoothly, no one is running out of anything, and so on.

6. Each booth will make some money. At the end of the day, pool all profits from each booth, pay whoever bought the prizes and supplies, and divide any money left over evenly among workers. If you like, you can decide to give the profits to a chosen charity—or just a few workers may decide to do this. If everyone wants to give the profits to charity, under all billboards and on the invitations write in small print: PROFITS WILL GO TO (name specific charity).

7. Keep trash baskets around. All workers clean up.

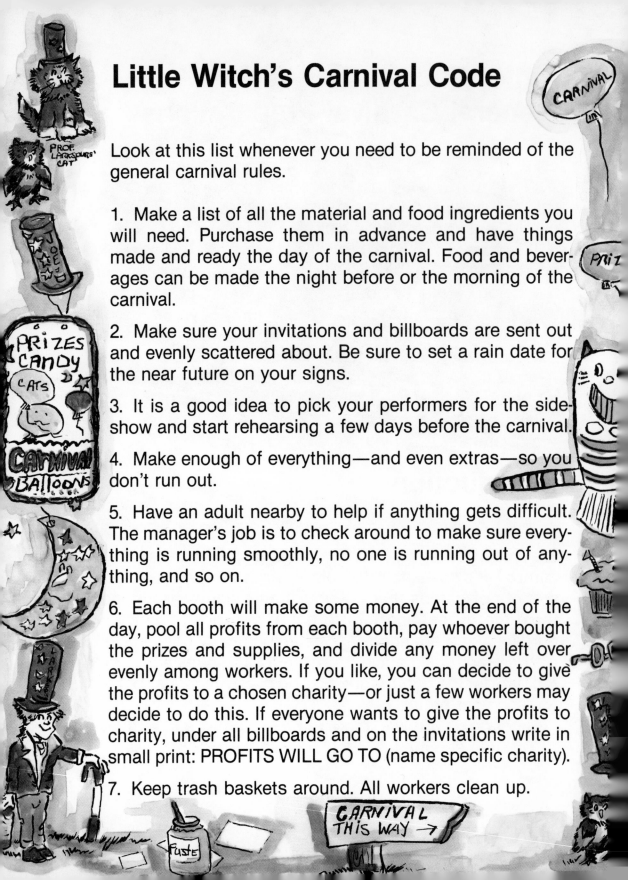

Little Witch's General Carnival Preparations

It's really pretty easy to put together a Little Witch's carnival. You need a few basic things, then follow directions carefully, and look at the pictures for ideas.

It is best to have the carnival outdoors. But if you can't, you can have it in the basement. Or if you live in an apartment, you can do two or three booths at a time and run it all week.

Six to eight friends to run the carnival are a good number. You need to make costumes, money boxes, hats, glasses, tickle sticks, food, and things to sell at the souvenir booth. Put the booths together the day before the carnival. Don't forget to purchase a few prizes—suggestions are given later. Now you're ready to go. It's easy!

Some of the things you will need are: lots of cartons of various sizes in good condition or small tables you have around the house or can borrow; poster board; light-colored construction paper; insulating plastic (from the hardware store) or artist's frosted acetate; masking tape; Elmer's glue, Duco cement, or rubber cement; stick-on stars; tempera paints; magic markers; tinfoil; crepe paper; string; straws; wooden dowels (from hardware store); paper plates; old fabrics; stew-type pot; brown grocery bags; flat rocks; balloons; stapler and staples; cardboard cylinders; scissors; plastic cups; food colors; empty cans and bottles; baskets; tennis balls.

TREE SIGNS (billboards)

Post them in town on trees or around the neighborhood. The Little Witch lives just inside the woods, so she posts them around her area.

To make a tree sign you need: 22″ × 28″ full-size poster board (white, pink, orange, or yellow). Cut each sheet in half to make two signs.

Round off the corners as in picture. Cut out on curved line.

Draw and cut moons, stars, and witches' hats out of 2½″ × 2½″ pieces of colored construction paper and tinfoil—a variety of each—and paste them all around sign as in the drawing.

Leave a big center space to write announcement, date, time, place, and so on with thick magic marker. If you decide to give your carnival profits to a charity, write this at the bottom. Make several and tack or nail wherever you think your friends will find them.

PERSONAL TALL HAT INVITATIONS

You will need 9″ × 12″ light-colored construction paper. Draw and cut out the shape of a tall hat. Here's how: Measure 2″ in from each side at middle and draw dots. From top measure 9½″ down and mark dots. From top draw straight lines connecting dots. Mark 2 slanted lines from bottom dots outward to end of paper. Connect ends with a curve that touches bottom of paper for hat brim.

Draw another curve for top of hat and paste tinfoil across top of brim for a hat band or use a different color paper. Paste small cutout stars on that if desired. Write your announcement on hat as in picture. Pass out or fold in half from top and place in mailboxes. Write FORTUNES, FUN, AND FOOD on card, plus date, time, and address. Include a rain date. If you've decided to give your profits to a charity, write this in small letters at the bottom.

TIN FOIL BAND→

COME TO:
A LITTLE
WITCH'S
CARNIVAL:
MAY 10-IN
FORTUNES
FUTURES
F·OOD
FUN

247 SWAMP Rd.
RAIN DATE: MAY 11
PROFITS TO CHARITY

GENERAL CARNIVAL WORKERS' COSTUMES

Gather together all the friends who will be running the carnival with you to get your costumes ready beforehand. Everyone must wear a carnival worker's costume. Each person needs a hat, jacket or cloak, glasses, cane, and funny shoes or tall boots. Choose a manager (carnival overseer).

TO MAKE HIGH HATS: All the hats are made the same. Everyone writes his or her name (or the carnival name they choose) on the front of the hat, except manager, who writes MANAGER in big letters down front so people will know where to go with a problem. He or she also pastes a big star on front of hat, cut out of tinfoil. Manager can also run a booth.

You will need 13″ × 14″ construction paper or poster board (orange, yellow, red, purple, or blue). Bend it into a cylinder. Overlap one end about an inch. Staple each end as far in as possible. Then tape seam closed. Next, you need a dinner-size paper plate. Paint it the same color as cylinder. Stand cylinder up on plate circle and trace brim. Cut out inner circle on traced lines, so cylinder slips tightly through plate.

Carefully insert cylinder through plate hole. Cut flaps ½″ × 1″ all around at bottom of cylinder. Cut on lines, not near staples. Bend flaps back to attach to plate. Staple securely. Staple to flap a 12″ piece of string to each side of cylinder to tie under chin. You can paste a 2″ × 13″ tinfoil band across bottom of hat. Put your name toward top of hat. Make one up, depending on what booth you are working, like "Little Good Luck Charlie," "Margie the Future Maker," and so on. Manager writes MANAGER down front in large print. Paste homemade stick-on stars all over your hat. Later on you will see how you can make variations in all your costumes.

STRINGS

GOOD LUCK CHARLIE

CARNIVAL
(NO FOXES ALLOWED)

CARNIVAL WORKER'S OUTFIT

You need an old suit jacket or blazer, one that is a little large for you—perhaps an older brother's or sister's. Wear dress gloves, any color, preferably white, pink, red, or beige. If you can, paste glitter, sequins, or 2″ × 2″ stars cut out of tinfoil or colored paper all over your jacket. Wear slacks or a long skirt, such as a Little Witch skirt (page 13). Wear high boots (slacks tucked in) or fancy shoes (dance shoes). Girls also can wear a suit jacket or they can wear a cloak instead (page 13) and be a Little Witch carnival worker.

The manager pins a big star cut out of a 3″ × 3″ square of colored paper or tinfoil on the front of his or her jacket, with MANAGER printed on it.

You can wear a high hat with the Little Witch's cloak and skirt if you like.

12

HOBNOB CANE

You need three cardboard cylinders from paper towel or tinfoil rolls, and one toilet-paper cylinder. Tape the three larger cylinders together with masking tape. Tape the small cylinder to top sideways as cane handle. If you tape it several times wrapped around, it will stay, or cut flaps around edge and tape those down. Cover entire cane with several layers of crepe paper glued down. Use a different color for each cylinder (pink, purple, yellow) or paint each area with temperas.

LITTLE WITCH ATTIRE

Some of you might want to dress as a Little Witch carnival worker. Wear funny socks (stripes or bright colors), old tall shoes or dark shoes, and a long skirt, such as a long flair slip (black or a very dark color) or a woman's skirt, so that it is long on you. Pin it or tie around  you with a belt or sash. Cloaks can be made from sheets, old fabric, or crepe paper. Cut out a large circle that will be big enough to cover your shoulders to waist. Cut a small inner circle, large enough for your head to fit through. Cut ¾ of the way up front, turn under about ½", and tape to under side of cape as seam. Paste stars and moons on this also. Wear high hat (page 10).

CLOAK PATTERN

13

520795

CARNIVAL BOOTHS

TO MAKE CARNIVAL BOOTHS: Carnival booths are easy to make. They are even easier if you can gather several old tables—then you don't have to make them at all, just cover the tables with cloth (tablecloth), crepe paper, or old pieces of fabric you have around. If you are making homemade booths, be sure they are sturdy. Have an adult help. Tape three large sturdy cartons together with masking or electrical tape. Cartons can be found at the grocery store. Put the cartons together and wrap the tape around them several times so they do not come apart. If the cartons are small you may need 6 to place one on top of the other for height. Cover with old sheets, fabric, or crepe paper. If you like, tape smaller cartons in back for supplies, secrets, prizes, and so on. Make a sign (follow directions for making billboards, page 8) to put in front telling the name of the game or type of food to be sold. Keep a wastebasket nearby and a sheet of paper with each booth's game rules.

EXTRA CARTONS

PAINT ON STARS AND MOONS

HOORAY!

WHEEL OF FORTUNE GAME

Carnival: TO YOUR RIGHT

TO MAKE MONEY BOXES: These can be made out of a cigar, shoe, or any box with a lid. Cover it with tinfoil or crepe paper, enough so writing doesn't show through. Paste small stars cut out of colored construction paper all over it. Write MONEY BOX on top with magic marker. This is where you keep the money you collect, and from which you give out change. Each booth has a money box.

TICKLE STICKS

For each tickle stick cut two 4″ × 4″ squares—one of colored paper and one of tinfoil. Staple foil to paper in center in 3 places. Cut 4 corner slits about 1¾″ long toward center, through both squares, about ¾″ wide. Fluff out the foil, shake it, and staple a straw to the back. These do not go in a circle but shake a bit in the wind. Tickle your friends with them. You may staple another cutout tinfoil to back if you want more fullness. Sell for 15¢.

STAPLE STRAW TO BACK CENTER

CARNIVAL WORKERS' COLORED GLASSES

You need insulating plastic, which comes in a roll or by the piece at the hardware store. (It is the plastic used to cover windows from drafts.) Or you can purchase artist's frosted acetate, which comes in large sheets or in a pad at the art store. You also need heavy cardboard (shirt backing) or poster board. All carnival workers wear glasses. Make several extra pairs to sell at the souvenir booth for 25¢.

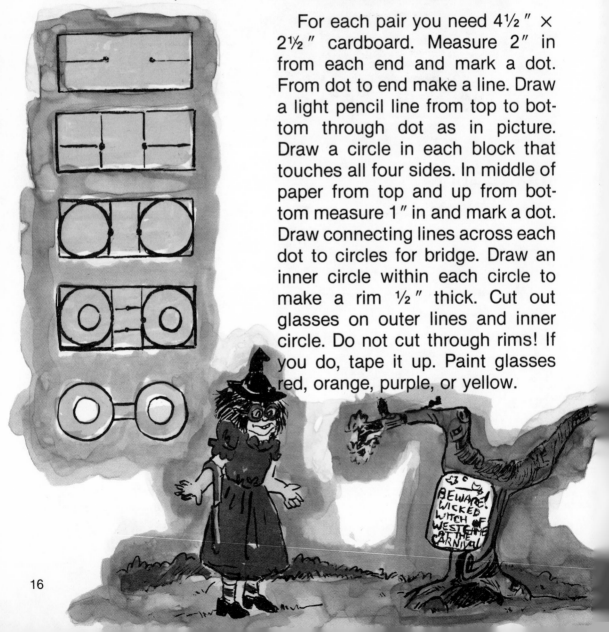

For each pair you need 4½ " × 2½ " cardboard. Measure 2" in from each end and mark a dot. From dot to end make a line. Draw a light pencil line from top to bottom through dot as in picture. Draw a circle in each block that touches all four sides. In middle of paper from top and up from bottom measure 1" in and mark a dot. Draw connecting lines across each dot to circles for bridge. Draw an inner circle within each circle to make a rim ½ " thick. Cut out glasses on outer lines and inner circle. Do not cut through rims! If you do, tape it up. Paint glasses red, orange, purple, or yellow.

BEWARE! WICKED WITCH OF WEST AT THE CARNIVAL

Cut a 2½″ × 4″ piece of plastic for each pair of glasses, or a piece large enough to cover circle in back. Staple securely to back in several places. (Be sure prongs of staples don't stick out!) Cut away excess. Color circle from back with yellow, red, orange, or purple magic marker (waterproof). Make sure the plastic you get holds marker colors. Mix and match colors—if outside of your glasses are purple, color the lens yellow.

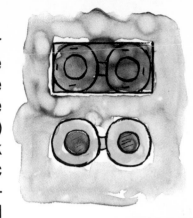

TO MAKE EYEGLASS HANDLES: You need 2 pieces of 4½″ × 1″ cardboard. For each, draw a lumplike mushroom near end, leaving about ¼″ from end and top as in picture. Cut out mushroom and discard. Bend a ½″ flap at other end and staple to eyeglass rim. Fold over ears. Tie strings through tiny holes punched at ends of handles to tie in back of head if glasses keep falling down. Or staple pipe cleaners to rims for handles.

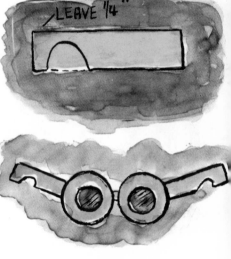

LEAVE ¼″

TO MAKE MARDI GRAS STYLE GLASSES: Staple one straw to one end of back of rim.

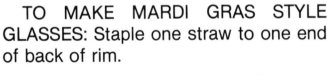

FORTUNES
FUTURES
GAME BOOTHS
PRIZES AND SOUVENIRS

SOUVENIR TRINKET BOOTH

This is the opening booth that displays the items for sale at the carnival. Try to make this the first booth as you enter the carnival. Don't forget to put up your sign. Sell your colored glasses, tickle sticks, rock cats, and witches' moons here. Be sure to put a small sign with the price of each item in front of the items, or write the items and prices all on the big sign. Make several of each—8 or 10. Get your friends who will be running the carnival to help you make things beforehand. Put the money you collect in your money box. Divide the earnings later. Cats and moons are 25¢; tickle sticks, 15¢; glasses, 25¢. Good luck!

GOOD LUCK ROCK CATS
AND HANGING WITCHES' MOONS (25¢)

These items are for sale at the souvenir booth and they are also used as prizes for some of the game winners, so make several of them. Attach a tag to the moon that says GOOD LUCK WITCH'S MOON. The cheshire cat is always grinning, so be sure to paint wide grins on the rocks and tag each CHESHIRE CAT.

TO MAKE MOONS: Cut a 10″ × 10″ square of cardboard or poster board. Draw a full circle on it. Cut out circle. Divide in half with pencil. Divide each half circle in half with a curved line as in picture, to have two quarter moons. Cut out on lines and discard inner oval. Keep two outer moons. Paint or cover with pink, yellow, or blue crepe or construction paper and stars cut out of tinfoil (glue down) or use stick-on stars. Paint eyes, nose, and smiling mouth if you want. Punch a hole at top corner and pull an 18″ string through. Tie closed in a knot. Hang anywhere.

TO MAKE ROCK CATS: Try to find smooth flat wide rocks. Scrub and dry them. Paint on eyes, nose, and whiskers with temperas. Cut triangle ears out of felt or construction paper to fit on head. Glue bottom to back of rock. Paint on a big cheshire cat grin with pink or red temperas.

WITCHES' WHEEL OF FORTUNE GAME (5¢)

This should be the first real game when your friends enter the carnival. Good luck or bad luck—they will now find out.

You need a large carton about 12″ × 24″ to stand on your table or carton stand. Thirty-dozen egg cartons are great and can be found at the grocery store. Ask the manager. Get a ¼″-wide dowel or thin curtain rod, about 20″ to 24″ long (wooden dowels can be purchased at the hardware store for about 40¢). A perfectly formed stick will do also.

Paint the box or cover it well with crepe paper or construction paper. You can paste on tinfoil stars, moons, and tall hats cut out of 3″ × 3″ pieces. Leave space open where wheel is to go. Stand carton up.

Measure about 8″ down from top of one side of the carton and mark a dot. Have an adult punch a hole with a scissor just enough for rod to fit through. Stick rod from side, through middle, to other side. Let it stick out about 3″. With masking tape, go around and over rod and tape well to carton. This is the front. Hold bottom of box down with a brick or books. Tape a large piece of construction paper down over open side as a curtain.

COVER TOP AND ONE SIDE

LEAVE A CLEAR SPACE

STICK OUT 3″ THIS WILL BE FRONT

ROD THROUGH SIDES OF CARTON

Out of a 9″ × 9″ square of light-colored poster board or cardboard, draw a circle that touches each end. You may need to double poster board for thickness. Cut out circle. Divide it in 6 parts as best you can with red or black magic marker. Number the parts in large letters. Punch a hole in middle of circle, just enough to fit over dowel. Make sure circle is small enough for symbols to fit around it on carton. Cut out of colored paper 1. large star, 2. witch's moon, 3. witch's hat, 4. cat's hat, 5. witch's brew pot, 6. candle. In a circle, as in picture, paste your symbols.

Player picks a number on wheel, say 4. Worker spins the wheel several times. When it stops, whatever symbol that number points to is the fortune prediction. Keep fortunes written with corresponding numbers on pieces of folded paper in a box. You need several copies of each fortune. When you run out, make more. The player gets to keep the paper with his or her fortune written on it.

SYMBOL PREDICTIONS: You can make up your own or use the Little Witch's.

Moon: If you establish high goals and dreams now, most will come true later.

Star: You will never be lonely—friends like your winning personality.

Cat: If a woman, you will be beautiful and lucky. If a man, handsome and prosperous.

Hat: If you go into your own business, you will do very well; may make a fortune

Candle: Good luck or bad luck—when it comes your way, you will handle it well.

Brew Pot: If you have a burning ambition, follow it through, and it will come true.

Be sure to put your sign out in front with bonus notice: Bonus: Players who hit the moon get a box of Cracker Jacks along with fortune. Workers also call out, "Come and get it. Hit the moon and win Cracker Jacks!"

PROFESSOR LARKSPUR'S
CRYSTAL CUP FUTURE GAME (5¢)

The Little Witch has a friend in the woods called Professor Larkspur (that is also the name of his cat). He is a bit of a medicine man and a sorcerer. The Little Witch learned this game from him. The person who works this booth can write PROFESSOR LARKSPUR on his or her tall hat.

You need several clear plastic cups (and refills if they get dirty), a set of food colors, a straw, tinfoil, two chairs or stools, and a pail of water. Cover your booth stand or table top with a tablecloth or material.

  MAKE MIXER WAND: Cut a star out of 3″ × 3″ tinfoil. Paste it on heavy paper. Staple a straw to center in back. This is your wand. Keep extra straws if one wears out.

FOOD COLORS: Player picks 2 food colors that he feels are his or her lucky colors. Professor Larkspur puts a drop of each color in a cup filled ¾ of the way with water and mixes and swirls this way and that with wand until water is blended. There may be variations of color depending on how many drops of each color are used. On next page is a general future color chart to use. Pretend you are studying the color. Then whatever color it turns out closest to, read the future from your chart. Make a chart and keep several copies of each color future on pieces of colored paper, so player can take his color future home. Use a new cup for each player. Charge 5¢. Can play as many times as they like.

PROFESSOR LARKSPUR'S CHART FOR FUTURES:

Green: Your future looks bright. Avoid looking for trouble!

Red: There is fame, but you must learn to listen.

Blue: Good luck will come shortly, but there will be obstacles.

Yellow: Your life will unfold like a jigsaw puzzle if you follow directions.

Lime: You have a tendency to take chances—be careful!

Pink: Stay calm, and you'll get what you need.

Brown: Future foggy. Try two new colors for free.

Purple: You might go in the theater or movies.

Orange: Danger—try later!

WITCHES' WISHING TELESCOPE PREDICTIONS (2¢)

Your friends make a wish or ask a question. The telescope predicts what the outcome will be. Charge 2¢ a wish. Put out a sign with the name of the game and the price in front of booth.

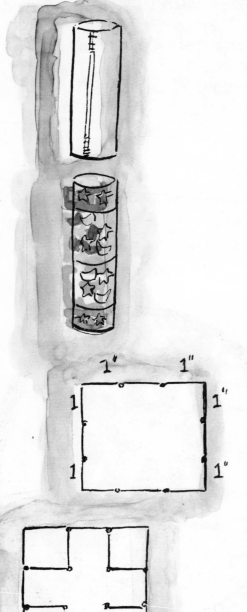

MAKE TELESCOPE: Cut a 10″ × 14″ piece of poster board. Roll it lengthwise into a cylinder. Overlap edge 1″. Staple and tape seam closed well. Cover with 3 different colors crepe or construction paper. Trace the bottom circle and put a piece of acetate or plastic on to cover it. Glue and tape it down well. Paste stick-on stars, cutout stars, and painted moons all over cylinder.

PREDICTION CUBE: Cut out a 3″ × 3″ poster board piece. Measure 1″ in from top on both ends and mark dots. Do the same on bottom and up and down sides. Measure 1″ down from top dots and mark dots. Connect to outer dots. Measure 1″ up from bottom dots. Connect to side dots. Make a middle square connecting dots as in picture on the next page.

Cut off the four outer corner blocks, as in drawing, and save one. In the five connected squares write a prediction, with dark pen or fine-tip marker. 1. Sorry, signs say no. 2. Ask me again. 3. Yes, it's true! 4. It looks good. 5. Most likely. Fold up box so predictions are on outside. Close sides with transparent tape. On the square you saved write: 6. Future foggy. Tape to open spot on cube. Put cube in telescope. Close open end of telescope, as you did other end, with acetate or plastic, traced to fit. Player makes a wish. Carnival worker shakes the telescope and turns it up and down several times, then places it straight up on table. Player peers in to see his or her prediction on cube. Players may try as many times as they like, at 2¢ a try.

WICKED WITCH OF THE WEST GAME (a game of skill)
10¢, two tries

In the story of the Wizard of Oz, there is an evil witch called the Wicked Witch of the West. In this game, the players try to knock her down. *You need:* 6 empty soda or soup cans. After you open the cans, cover the open end with tinfoil and tape it down around can with masking tape. Then cover cans with orange or yellow construction paper. On one can, draw or paint a witch figure in black, as in picture. Stack up the cans in a pile: 3 on bottom, 2 on top of them, and one (the witch) on top. Players stand 3 feet behind booth and try to knock the cans or just the witch can down with a tennis ball. The object is to make the witch on top fall. If she falls, the player wins a prize. Each player gets two tries for 10¢. They can win a candy from potluck hat or a balloon. (Buy a bag of balloons and write messages on them with magic marker: GOOD LUCK, YOU'RE GREAT, PEACE, HAPPINESS, I'M FOR CATS, and so on. When they blow it up, the message will expand.) Write prizes on your sign with price of game in front of booth. Have tickets that say, "1 Free Potluck Candy."

WITCH SHAPE

OWL AND MOUSE (FISHING LUCK) GAME 20¢ a try

Put out your sign. The owl plays against the mouse. One player chooses to be the owl, one the mouse. First prepare the hats. Player must wear a game hat. *You need:* an 18″ × 1″ strip construction paper or poster board. Form a band shape and staple closed in three places. Now make owl and mouse ears. *You need:* four 3″ × 3″ squares of brown or orange construction paper. On 2 squares draw a circle that touches 4 ends, for round mouse ears. On 2 squares draw a triangle with a point that touches top and one point in each bottom corner. Cut out on lines. Staple ears to back of band. Make an extra hat of each, in case one tears. Owl slips on owl hat, mouse wears mouse hat.

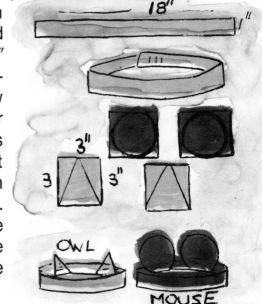

GAME TAKES PLACE BEHIND THE BOOTH: You need two flat boards, heavy cardboard, or plywood, each one at least 11″ × 14″, small empty soda bottles, 2 to 2½′ poles for fishing rods (can use sticks, curtain rods, dowels), 2 to 3′ pieces of cord, thin rope, or heavy string.

Have an adult help you. Tie a loop at one end of the cord, large enough to fit nicely over top half of bottle. Use bottle as measurement guide. Tie other end of cord to end of fishing pole rod. Place each bottle lying down toward top of flat board. Each player gets a fishing pole. Two play at once.

OBJECT: He or she must try to get the loop of the cord over the bottle top and slowly stand bottle up on board. The first to do it is the winner and gets a prize.

CLUES: Slip the loop over the bottle carefully, slide it down a bit, and slowly stand it up. Once it is up, hold it still with loop over it. Don't pull cord off. Object is just to have bottle in standing position. Who will win? Either the owl or the mouse. Keep a clock or a watch handy. Players get 10 minutes to try their skill each game. Winners get: 1 free food choice at food booths or colored carnival glasses or a rock cat or witch's moon. (Make extras.) Give winners a colored paper that says "1 . . . . . . free" and write choice on ticket.

BALL IN BASKET GAME (a game of skill) 10¢ a try

You need 3 different-size baskets. The Little Witch uses a wood bushel basket, a tomato basket, and a small wicker basket. Set your baskets up next to one another (about a foot apart) in a line about 4 feet behind booth. Player gets 3 tennis balls. He or she must try to get a ball in each basket. If he gets each ball in a basket, he wins the big prize. If he gets 2 out of 3 in each basket, wins small prize. *Big prize:* 1 crunchy popcorn and a balloon. *Small prize:* a carnival cupcake.

Put out your sign with price and prizes on it in front. If player wins, give him a small slip of colored paper that says, "WINNER—1 Carnival Cupcake FREE" or "WINNER—1 Crunchy Popcorn FREE."

TRICKY DICE GAME (double your money)

Need a pair of dice. Get 3 cardboard pieces, each 2½″ × 7″. Lay out pieces at one end of booth. Write ODD on one piece, EVEN on another, and 7 on last piece in large letters with magic marker. Carnival worker keeps a supply of pennies, nickels, and dimes in booth's money box. Player picks

a card choice, ODD, EVEN, or 7 and places a coin (penny, nickel, or dime) on it. Worker rolls the dice. If it comes out in even numbers and player has coin on EVEN card, worker doubles player's money.

If it comes out ODD or 7, and player has coin on EVEN card, worker wins money. Object is to guess how the dice will turn out after rolled—ODD, EVEN, or 7—and place coin on proper card. If you win, you double your money. If you lose, worker gets it. Odd numbers are 3-5-9-11; even, 2-4-6-8-10-12; 7 is a total of seven dots on dice.

SURPRISE WITCH BURGERS (25¢)

Everyone usually wants to have a snack sooner or later. The Little Witch, the Goblin, and Professor Larkspur have been up all night preparing the treats. Make food stands the same as game stands. Keep your burgers in a cooler nearby. Only display a few at a time on a platter. Charge 25¢ for each. Put out your sign with price on it.

Bittersweet Burger Relish

6 small dill pickles	4 stalks finely chopped celery
1 cup mayonnaise	2 Tbsps. sugar or sweetener
1 Tbsp. lemon juice	

Chop pickles super small, add mayonnaise and other ingredients. Mix all up well. You may need to add more mayonnaise, depending on your taste. Keep extra ingredients inside, in case you have to make another batch. Prepare your relish-filler the night before. In morning, put on your burgers and wrap each in plastic wrap. Refrigerate.

For Each Burger Follow This Formula:

1 burger bun	1 slice bologna or cheese
handful of sprouts	2 or 3 tsps. bittersweet relish

Put the bologna or cheese on one side of the bun, then sprouts, and top with relish. Close bun.

Try to get orange or yellow napkins. Keep small paper plates and plastic forks nearby in case someone needs them. You can use store-bought relish instead of the Little Witch's formula. If someone wants a devil dog instead of a witch burger, here's how to make them:

Devil Dogs (25¢)
Put one slice of bologna rolled up on a hot dog roll. Top with sprouts, 2 Tbsps. burger relish, and a light layer of ketchup. Close bun.

OLD WITCH'S CORN COBLETS (10¢)
AND CRUNCHY POPCORN (10¢)

The oldest witch in the neighborhood suggested these for the Little Witch's carnival.

Corn Coblets (10¢)
Boil several ears of corn. Drain. Have an adult cut each ear in three places for 3 tiny pieces. Serve on a large platter with a melted butter dip in a bowl next to it. Keep salt handy. Put a colored toothpick in each coblet. You can keep butter fresh on ice in your cooler. For anyone daring enough, do as Old Witch —she dips her coblet lightly in ketchup after the butter.

Old Witch's Crunchy Popcorn (10¢)

½ cup melted butter   ½ cup honey
3 quarts popped popcorn 1 cup chopped nuts
   (freshly popped or store
   bought, already pre-
   pared)

You need an adult to help: Preheat oven to 350°. Blend butter and honey together while heating gently. Mix the popcorn with nuts and pour the honey/butter mixture over it. Mix well. Spread a thin layer on a cookie sheet. Bake 15″, till crispy-looking. Yields about 3 qts. broken-up nut crunch. Wrap in portions in plastic wrap.

WITCHES' COOL BREWS STAND (10¢)

This can be run by the same person who runs the burger stand. Don't forget to put a big poster-board sign in front of each stand with the name, prices, prizes, free things, etc.

Cool Brews Stand

You need a large bag of round pretzels and small paper cups. A guest gets one free pretzel with the purchase of a cool brew. Keep lots of ice in your brew and a cooler of it nearby for refills.

Apple Iced Tea

Makes 8 cups: Mix 4 cups of regular prepared tea or herb or Red Zinger and 4 cups apple juice. Add sugar if needed and mix well.

Goblin's Rainbow Punch

This is one of the Goblin's favorite brews. It mixes well with the carnival cupcakes on the next page.

       3 cups pineapple juice
       2 cups orange juice
       1 cup strawberry or cherry soda

Mix all together and stir gently. Serve from large jugs, jars, or pitchers.

GOBLIN'S SPICY CARNIVAL CUPCAKES (15¢)

The Goblin is a chef in his spare time, so he makes his special cupcakes for the carnival. This recipe makes 18. If you think you will have more guests or if some want doubles, make another batch.

Goblin's Spicy Applesauce Cupcakes

1½ cups sifted white flour	½ cup brown sugar
3 tsps. baking powder	2 eggs, lightly beaten
1 tsp. cinnamon	1 cup applesauce
½ tsp. nutmeg	½ cup milk
½ tsp. salt	¼ cup oil

The goblin adds ½ cup wheat germ or crunchy granola to the mixture for good health.

Sift together flour, baking powder, cinnamon, nutmeg, and salt in a large bowl. Stir in brown sugar. Mix eggs, applesauce, milk, and oil in a small bowl. Add the wheat germ or cereal and mix. Add to dry ingredients. Stir just a few times to moisten. Spoon batter into greased muffin tins ⅔ full. Bake at 400° for about 20 minutes, or until toothpick inserted in center comes out clean. Let cool. Optional: spread with marmalade.

POTLUCK CANDY (15¢)

Here are two very sweet candy recipes. Make several pieces of each. Wrap in waxed paper or plastic wrap and put them in an upside-down carnival worker's hat. Write POTLUCK on the hat in big letters with magic marker. Guests pay 15¢ and reach in the hat, not knowing which treat they will get. If they want the other one, they have to try again and pay another 15¢.

Goblin's Nutty Light Fudge

½ cup nonfat milk solids   ½ cup peanut butter
1 cup shredded coconut   ½ cup peanuts, chopped
½ cup sunflower seed   ¼ cup honey
   kernels   ½ cup sesame seeds
¼ cup water

Combine all ingredients in a very large bowl and mix well until mixture sticks together. Press into a flat buttered pan. Cut into small squares and wrap in waxed paper or plastic wrap. Store in refrigerator until day of carnival. Makes one pound.

Professor Larkspur's 1, 2, 3, Easy Magic Granola Candy

honey   shredded coconut   crunchy granola

Add enough honey and coconut to granola to make it stick together. Start with about 3 cups granola, ¼ cup honey, and ½ cup coconut. Keep adding a little more honey and coconut until you have the right amount of everything and it sticks together well. Form into little balls and wrap in waxed paper. These can be for sale at the cupcake booth or a separate booth.

LITTLE WITCH'S SPOOKY POPS (20¢ a pop)

These are very refreshing—they taste like real ice cream. You have to keep them in a cooler, but put your sign out in front of the booth. Keep a few out on display on a plate. Make about 18, unless you anticipate a larger sale. Keep cooler on hand.

YOU NEED: Wooden skewers or ice cream sticks, bananas, honey, and shredded coconut (comes packaged or in a can). Peel bananas. Brush well with honey. Then roll in a plate of shredded coconut, to look like a ghost. If you like, stick two gumdrops, chocolate bits, or raisins near top for eyes. Carefully insert sticks. Put bananas on a tray lined with foil and cover with foil. Freeze until firm. Take out in time for hungry carnival guests.

INSERT SKEWER AT END bEFORE FREEZING L.W.

SIDESHOW

SHOW TIME: Performing Animal Sideshow (10¢)

Late in the afternoon toward the end of the carnival, the Little Witch and her friends put on an animal sideshow. Choose the carnival workers who are talented in singing, dancing, acrobatics, music, stand-up comics, magicians, and so on for this show. Select a barker—he or she is the one who lures the guests to the show, saying things like, "Step right up. See the talking dog and the dancing bear. Watch the owl stand on his head. Admission is only 10¢, but you'll never forget the sights." The barker wears a carnival worker's costume and uses the hobnob cane to point out the acts. Make the costumes and practice the acts a few days before the carnival. Bring the costumes to the carnival with you. If someone in the show also runs a booth, get the manager or someone else to look after it while the show is going on. The barker comes out and introduces the first act. The show consists of three acts: 1. The Singing Hoot Owl, 2. The Performing Dog, 3. The Dancing Bear.

SHOWTIME!
4:00 P.M
UNBelievable
ACTS
Dancing BEAR
TALKiNg Dog
CRAZY OWL
SideShow 10¢

42

HOOT OWL COSTUME

To be the owl make the owl hat on page 29. Use these directions for the band of the other animal hats. Darken the outer areas around your eyes with brown or black cake eye shadow. Be careful not to rub it in your eyes. Wash off later with soap and water. Fluff your hair out or attach several 4″ × 1″ strips crepe paper (brown or orange) along hat band for feathers. Color nose with yellow food coloring for beak. Wear a brown, orange, or gray sweater or sweatshirt. Underneath it tie a small pillow to your middle with a rope or belt. For a dressy owl wear a vest. Wear slacks, old pants, tights with pedal pushers, or shorts (same color as top). Wear brown, yellow, or orange socks on your hands and feet.

OWL WINGS: You need 4 pieces of 18″ × 9″ yellow, brown, or orange construction or poster paper. Measure 15″ down from top. Draw a light pencil line across paper. Draw 3 points that touch bottom in a row in the space. Cut out on lines. Make 4 wings. Pin one wing along top of arm and across chest. Pin another wing underneath arm and across chest. Do the same with other arm.

TAIL FEATHERS: Make same as one wing. Pin to seat of pants. For thick tail feathers attach two or three wings, one on top of the other.

OWL FEET: You need 6″ × 6″ yellow, brown, or orange construction paper. To make ankle, measure 2″ from each side at top and mark a dot. Measure 2″ down from each dot, mark dot. Connect top dots to bottom with lines. Make 3 V-shaped claw points, as in picture—one on each side  that touches end of paper and one down center to bottom. Cut out on lines. Pin ankle in 2 places over your sock for feet.

The owl sings and hoots, dances, and plays an instrument, if possible. Instruments can be real instruments if any carnival workers have them or paper towel cylinders with 5 holes cut along the top, or a spoon and tin can, or a whistle. Have two owls in the show if you like.

PERFORMING DOG COSTUME

If you want to be a dog with patches on his eyes, color around your eyes the same as for hoot owls. Blacken your nose. Make the head band same as owl's, except attach floppy ears to it, or pin your hair under an old wool cap and pin ears to side. Wear white, black, or brown sweater or sweatshirt and same color pants. Wear white, black, or brown socks on hands and feet, or one white, other brown, for spotted dog. (Sweatsuits and joggers' outfits make good tops and/or bottoms for animal costumes.)

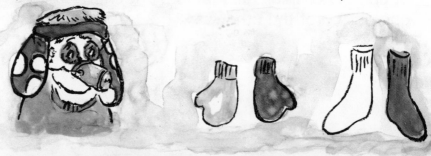

MAKE EARS: Need two 5″ × 7″ brown or black construction paper pieces. Make an ovallike shape or loop on it as in picture. Pin or staple cutout ear to your band or cap. Paint white spots on ears, if spotted dog. All animals can wear carnival glasses, to be more glamorous.

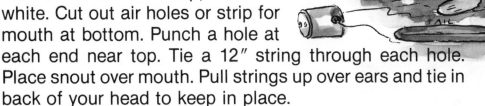

DOGGIE'S SNOUT: You need a 4 or 6 oz.-size coffee cup, brown or white. Cut out air holes or strip for mouth at bottom. Punch a hole at each end near top. Tie a 12″ string through each hole. Place snout over mouth. Pull strings up over ears and tie in back of your head to keep in place.

TAIL: Fill a thin sock with fabric, tissues, or cotton. Pin ankle part of sock to back. Or fill a 9″ × 3″ piece of crepe paper with cotton or tissue. Tape closed. Pin to pants for tail. Paint spots on it if desired.

The dog dances or does a jig. Barker tells him to roll over, go through a hoop, perform tricks, acrobatics, balance an acorn or small object on snout cup. He can also tell jokes and perform a magic trick. Do a hula.

DANCING BEAR COSTUME

The bear wears a big pillow tied to his middle, the same as the owl. His costume is all brown (or all white for a polar or Russian dancing bear)—a big old furry sweater is good to wear over the pillow. Try to wear a pair of furry mittens or heavy brown or white socks on hands and feet, or furry slippers.

Blacken eye area and nose. The bear gets a snout like the dog. Make it the same way, except paint it brown or cover it with brown paper. (Unless it's a white bear, then leave white and paint bottom black.)

TO MAKE EARS: Make the headband the same as owl but cut 2 small circles out of a 3″ × 3″ square of brown construction paper. Staple at bottom to back of band. Wear over your head for ears.

The bear dances (ballet is fine), eats honey, tells a story, and sings a bear song (if you have one). Use your hobnob cane during the act.

The show goes on around 4 o'clock. Have all your costumes ready. The barker wears the carnival worker's costume. At the end all the animals come out and perform at once, like a 3-ring circus.

46

WITCHES' BREW-POT RAFFLE (tickets, 5¢)

The carnival guests can purchase their raffle tickets at any time during the carnival. You need a small stand and a large pot in which to put the tickets. Don't forget to put out your raffle sign in front. The raffle winner is called off at the end of the carnival.

TO MAKE TICKETS: You need a ruler, pencil, and construction paper. With your ruler and a pencil draw lines across the paper one inch apart. Mark off with ruler and pencil every 2″. Cut out on lines, so that each ticket is 2″ long. Fold each piece in half. Write the same number on each half, starting from 1 and continuing in order, for each piece. When player purchases a ticket, tear in half. Give player one half and put the other half, folded, in the brew pot. At the end of the carnival, announce that the raffle will be drawn. Stir the pot well with a big spoon or your cane. Choose someone and have her close eyes and pick a ticket out of the pot. Player holding the other half wins. Prize is the cheshire cat.

CHESHIRE CAT (50¢)

In the story *Alice in Wonderland*, the striped Cheshire Cat was always grinning and had a lot of wisdom. The Little Witch makes these for her friends at the carnival. You can sell them at the souvenir booth for 50¢ and use them as prizes.

THIS WAY OUT →

47

TO MAKE CAT: You need a white, gray, or black sock. Stuff out the toe and heel with tissues, cloth, foam, or clean old nylon stockings. Tie it closed tightly at the ankle with string. Cut out two 1″ square pieces of cardboard or poster board. Draw a triangle on each as in picture. Paint

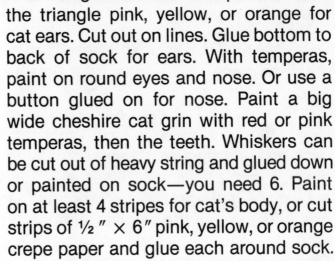

the triangle pink, yellow, or orange for cat ears. Cut out on lines. Glue bottom to back of sock for ears. With temperas, paint on round eyes and nose. Or use a button glued on for nose. Paint a big wide cheshire cat grin with red or pink temperas, then the teeth. Whiskers can be cut out of heavy string and glued down or painted on sock—you need 6. Paint on at least 4 stripes for cat's body, or cut strips of ½″ × 6″ pink, yellow, or orange crepe paper and glue each around sock.

TAIL: Cut a 2″ × 6″ piece of pink, orange, or yellow crepe paper and fill it with tissues or cotton. Tape closed well. Staple one end to back of cat for tail. Punch 2 holes near top of sock (head). Pull an 18″ string through it. Tie closed in a knot. Hands can be 2 cotton balls glued down, a few inches below grin. Hang cat anywhere you like for good luck; ask it a question when you need wisdom; keep it around to scare off evil spirits. Put a tag on it: CHESHIRE CAT.

Grade: 2-5